Polite to Bees

Polite to Bees

A Bestiary by Diana Hartog

*For Janice —
with love and good
wishes! Diana Hartog
june 7 1996*

Coach House Press
toronto

© Diana Hartog, 1992

Published with the assistance of the Canada Council, the Ontario Arts Council, and the Ontario Ministry of Culture and Communications.

Author's acknowledgements: Some of these pieces appeared previously in *The Malahat Review, Conjunctions, Prism, New West,* on the CBC program 'Speaking Volumes' and in the International Poetry Series, Northern Lights Publishers, London, England.
My thanks to the Ontario Arts Council, the British Columbia Cultural Services Branch, and the Canada Council.
My thanks also to Margaret Hartley—for her artistry, inspiration, and friendship.

The quotation from T.H. White's *The Book of Beasts* is reprinted by permission of the author and the Watkins/Loomis Agency.
Cover painting courtesy John Norris.

Canadian Cataloguing in Publication Data
Hartog, Diana
   Polite to bees

Poems.
ISBN 0-88910-417-4

1. Bestiaries – Poetry. I. Title.

PS8565.A77P64 1992   C811'.54   C92-095098-1
PR9199.3.H349P64 1992

Contents

9... The World Serpent
10... Mosquito
11... Sardines & Starlings
12... Spider
13... The Odalisque, Extinct
15... Snake
17... Butterfly
18... Sturgeon
19... Griffin
20... A Fish Story
22... Lambs
23... Dragons
24... Dik-Dik
25... The Edwardian Elephant Seal
29... Cruelty to Animals
30... A Working Elephant
31... The Cow
32... Women
33... Worm
34... Two Birds, One Stone
39... Moth
40... Men
41... Spider Web
42... The Fox, the Rabbit, the Duck
43... Lepus the Hare
44... The Crab of Logic
46... The Wrung Neck of a Swan
48... The Great Blue Heron
49... Intelligence in the Kingdom
51... An Elk, Still Thinking
52... Wild Turkey
53... Another Beast
54... Polite to Bees
55... Bats
56... Man-Eating Tigers
58... Scottie Dogs
60... The Albino Parrot
62... Red Flyer
63... Animals Lower Down in the Conversation
65... A Common Parasite
66... Right Front
68... Wart-Hog
69... Hart-Royale
70... The Gold Horn
73... The Dog Who Will Make All the Difference
74... The Black Bull
75... The Great Shape-Shifter

The Bestiary is a compassionate book .... It is polite to bees, it is tender to the poor, the horse moves it ....
T.H. White, *The Bestiary: A Book of Beasts*

The World Serpent

On the cabin wall above the stove, a tear of ruby glass sits in its bracket. On its bald red dome, dust has gathered; preserved inside is the antidote to fire. The liquid sealed within the ruby tear is distilled from human sorrow due to fire. Victims were paid to weep while they contemplated all they had lost to flame and smoke; they wept into a sterile bucket.

USE ONLY IN CASE OF FIRE, reads a brass plaque under the red glass tear. In which case, be sure when you throw it that you aim at the base of the fire—at the blue, hissing stem of the reptilian brain.

The fact that fire is a reptile has long been known: cold-blooded, able to regenerate any limb we might extinguish. Its tongue can extend for miles, and will feed far beyond hunger. A fire, once manifested, can grow or shrink in an inkling. It changes shape even as you look. Blink, and it has scattered like so many lizards. Grab the broom, you are looking up at the many heads of the Serpent, the hot breath from each maw burning your cheeks, singeing your hair.

And yet we invite fire into the house. We coax it with crumpled newspaper, with kindling; and strike a match to show the polite, curious creature exactly where to enter. The tiny black hole in the paper grows larger, a flame rises, looks around, all neck. It's here, fire.

We treat it like a pet, knowing its preferences, feeding it three small logs at a time. And we watch it. We sit and watch the darling. And when it's gone we say it has died.

Mosquito

Long suspected to be a product of human nature, the mosquito has been traced to the pineal—a ductless gland which rides a tiny saddle of bone astride the brain. Filled with the minuscule grit meant to irritate the ego, the pineal grinds these facts down to size, to a fine point, a technicality.

And then projects it wherever we happen to look.

Hypothetical, the mosquito will stray distracted, topic to topic, yet always wend its way back, within earshot. A seemingly easy prey, naked to the visible eye, its legs dangle down limply in space (like the thin pair of legs seen dangling from a window ledge, four floors up). To repeat: the mosquito exists at an indeterminate point, moot, usually in the middle of the night. There it trails a banner of sound, a thin vibrating wire; a gossamer of German steel, tautologic, argued round and round the furnished room.

It persists, this acid whine—near, then far, then near, drifting above the troubled brow of the sleeper. He stirs, moaning. And begins to *slap!* ... *slap!* at his face, his forehead, his hair; boxing his own ears, innocent, innocent.

Sardines & Starlings

I

Sardines swim in schools, yet never learn to count, or read music; they are Living Music, masters of the jazz riff as thousands tack to and fro, dodging between the lines and nets which dangle to catch them, fathoms down.

To speak of *a* sardine, in the singular, is inaccurate, even cruel. Separate, they lose direction, forget who they are, and what they were playing.

Whereas, *I! I! I!* they proclaim when thirty and forty thousand strong, flitting down the strait in a zig-zag, Wave to Particle to Wave.

The key number here is ten. In groups smaller than ten, sardines count only as food. (The key here being one of the slotted kind, which pirouettes around corners as it opens a tin of them swimming in oil.) When ten or less in number, sardines can no longer entertain higher equations; there's no critical mass—to feel joy, to work up a rhythm, to consider the tides, *Whither? Why?*

II

Starlings learn by repetition, the swing of the beat. In essence lyric, 'of the lyre,' hundreds of these birds will perch on a line strung between telephone poles. Starlings, starlings, all with heads cocked, as if listening for a call, for a certain mood to be plucked along the wire—at which they'll spring into the air and swirl in gyres of seemingly random notes.

Again, starlings cannot function in units less than ten.

Ten starlings will fit in a pie nicely. Starlings love the circle, so arrange them so, in radiating spokes, heads to the centre of the pie: they prefer their beaks to be touching, when forced to sing.

Spider

Spiders fell from the towel as her mother dried her from the bath; black widows, who held to their abdomens red violins which they never played; they liked moisture, they liked the damp folds of linens stolen by her father from motels.

In the attic, as she turned the page, a tarantula in hibernation emerged from a *National Geographic* covered with dust.

In school, she couldn't spell SPIDER without breaking the pencil lead. She learned that spiders possess eight limbs, as does a boy when pinning his girl to a shuddering web. Shovels, bricks, rolled-up newspapers; the broom, a two-by-four: she learned to kill.

In her purse now when going out she carries a hammer.

Sometimes a wad of tissue works best—when a spider, thirsty, has crept from the unconscious overnight, and is found trapped in the morning in the bathroom sink. Only the delicate daddy-longlegs does she save, scooping him to a piece of paper, to be erased outside. Outside lives the wolf spider, with a grey body the size of a mouldy grape which pops as the two-by-four smacks down.

To kill a spider shifts the weather; she doesn't care.

Married a week, she climbs to the attic with a heavy rock; and leaning out, lets it plummet towards the spider suddenly tensed on the path below.

Of all Creation, only spiders and humans realize they will die. Spiders know when.

But they keep coming. Drawn from the safety of the woods towards the porch steps, and the gutter pipe, up. Drawn to the larger than life *meaning* she seems to give them; to the moment when, scuttling towards her bed, they catch her eye: that thrilling scream of recognition.

The Odalisque, Extinct

The Odalisque reclines, rarely stands, and is never painted in stride. The feet do not support. The knees are sometimes bent akimbo as she lies at her length on a couch. This posture invites shadows to slowly approach.

The shadows of Paris are renowned—even more, perhaps, than its light. In April, fleet cumulus clouds sweep their shadows across the cobblestones; a broom leans its shadow against a wall at a pleasing slant; the shadows of strangers are trampled underfoot. These are the public shadows of Paris. To study the more private, one must move indoors, to the habitat of the Odalisque, circa 1923.

It is afternoon, after lunch and several wines. Angling in from the skylight, a shadow moves slowly across the floor of the studio; and will soon climb the shabby brocade of the couch and the fringe of black tassels dangling from a shawl.

All this takes time.

In the pose of the Odalisque, other shadows have already gathered. In the crook of her arm. In the hollow of her upturned palm. They nestle along her nakedness like privileged pets (the kind Parisiennes dine with on their laps, feeding them choice scraps from the table). Beneath her breasts smile two crescent moons of shadow. Her expression remains sober. Her nipples, impassive, return the turgid, unblinking stare of the voyeur. (The eyes of an Odalisque rarely meet one's gaze. There are exceptions—an 'Olympia' for instance—but most glance away, in order to think, or read.)

High on the Odalisque's cheekbone is dabbed a mole—to balance the drop of shadow which pools in her navel and threatens to spill over her rounded belly if she moves. And if the pubis is shorn, and the Odalisque's hand is not in the way, the tip of the brush will be dipped into black: and a fine delicate stroke, applied with a slight tremor, will part the lips.

The band of black encircling her throat is not a shadow but a black velvet ribbon, an artistic device implying the disjunction of head from body. It's a joke; in English it's called a choker.

A ribbon which, if missing from the canvas, Matisse has surely filched; and carries wadded in his pocket, fingering the velvet as he thinks about tomorrow, what he will change.

Snake

When suspended from the ceiling, a snake's carcass serves as a repellent against spiders.

Not so, the reverse; for a snake's interest, once aroused, is difficult to cure.

Consider that snake met in a vivarium in Paris, in a little building, mossy and antiquated, set off to one side in the Jardin des Plantes.

It cost nothing to enter, and shuffle with other couples past the glass cases, set flush into the walls. Hand in hand, newlyweds, filing past the *oxybele brilliant,* a snake as slim as your bride's pinkie-finger but chartreuse. Past a beige viper with pupils of opal, tired: the viper lies camouflaged to sand, having traced the loops of both your initials, over and over, over his square of desert.

Now the python—filling his picture window.

With her free hand, your love taps the glass. Nothing happens. Patience is needed, and the faith, as her fingernail taps at the coiled mass pressing close, that the python is alive. Wound around a bare, introduced branch, the huge reptile poses motionless within a painted jungle *à la* Rousseau. The head itself—beyond price, a Fabergé egg—is hidden, tucked away, there is nothing to think.

Just rest. Play dead. Pretend, along with the woman who's tapping, that the glass will hold.

Tap-tap ... tap-tap.

Slowly you stir, and the tableau vivant *cracks as you shift within your scales. The paint flakes as you stretch, and your head—perfectly chilled—levitates, to hatch a curious forked tongue. You begin to speak; of your childhood, of beatings. Of being hung from the ceiling. You grope for words, your tongue flicks nervously... In gratitude you embrace your stunned listener; but tenderly, gently, for tears fill her eyes. Soon she is sobbing openly—she understands! And you squee-eeze tighter, to console.*

And then it's over, the past, something to be shed. You loosen within your own skin, shrink from any touch.

'What's wrong?' you ask, as your bride shrugs off your arm. 'Nothing's *wrong*,' she replies, moving on to the next exhibit.

Butterfly

Another butterfly sails in slow motion over the neighbour's fence, to alight on the widower's bald knee and pant there, its two matching wings kissing, kissing, kissing to make up. Up to the last, he and his wife had this same pattern, warring for hours inside the shuttered house; then to stumble out into the garden hand in hand, dazed.

Take the fight next door: silent for the moment. The newly-weds are probably squared off at opposite sides of the kitchen, with sunlight pooled between them on the floor, deceptively shallow; neither will take the first step.

Usually it was he who spoke first, after months of speaking through the children: his formal, 'Tell your mother I won't be home for dinner,' to her cool, 'Tell your father the Buick won't start.' But then a word would slip out. He'd forget; he'd be passing her in the narrow hall on his way in to shave, and forget they weren't speaking. Colour would flush to her cheeks, she'd nod or something, and it would be over.

A fight is a delicate subject, laced with expletives, the bruises yellowing from their first purple bloom. And bone thin! fragile as bone-thin china, the shards transparent when held to the light.

Take this monarch's wing ... *He squints up at the sun while still eavesdropping, trying to piece together the broken voices from next door.* You'll often find them: a single wing torn off somehow; one of a pair of mute, rheumy eyes that used to blink about the flowers.

Sturgeon

Rumours of sturgeon feed miles down, along the bottom of northern lakes. For this species, death is final and appears as a great blinding sun at which they gape, ascending, reeled up on shore by a team of horses.

But life is lived in the dark.

Twenty feet long and gunmetal grey, the sturgeon swim among schools of sunken locomotives—old steam engines which have flung themselves off the end of the line, to lie tilted on their sides, breathing deeply through their gills; they can't move, their single headlamps angle off with fixed stares into the watery murk.

The sturgeon glide through these beams.

They circle the sooted stacks; nudge the front grills which once strained the landscape through slots. At the sprung doors of the fireboxes, still warm, the sturgeon hover. They nibble at the live glowing coals—a delicacy wrung from them in turn by fishermen, for the market; where gourmets buy the bright red eggs of the locomotives in jars, to spread on toast.

Griffin

From the mother's hindquarters, a tiny white claw emerges: tests for footing. One vestigial wing works free; then the other wing, as with a last contraction a tail follows and the window falls shut behind.

The janitor passes down the hall.

A thin membrane encases the intruder, a nylon-stocking-cap which the griffin himself tears open with his beak. There rises a moist pungent odour, as when an egg is rapped and thumbed open, the yolk spreading broken in the dish.

Licked clean, any evidence swallowed by his mother, the griffin advances quickly, fluffs the feathers along his spine. Soon, chained to his desk, he is handling gold: gold futures, gold certificates, golden nest eggs.

Years pass. He sits bent, stoop-shouldered, at his desk. Consulting his gold watch, he continues work. Poor posture, stunted wings, a squint: slowly the griffin turns to stone. And is lifted by crane to the top of the office tower; there to grip with petrified claws, and grimace down at the brokers far below, sunning on their lunch hour, their collars loosened.

A Fish Story

Hannibal decided he was old enough to catch a fish story.

'It was this long!' he exclaimed, and stretched wide his small freckled arms, as if to embrace a fat grandmother's thighs.

But skinny and tall and tight-lipped, she replied, 'You may tell stories all you want, but young boys must be ready to sacrifice flesh for fibs.' And she marched him out to the garage and handed him a hoe—the same hoe his grandfather wielded to *hack! ... hack!* at anything in the garden he couldn't name. 'For your punishment,' pronounced the grandmother, 'you are to saw off an inch from this handle.'

Hannibal took his time, scanning the rows of tools, and chose finally the keyhole saw, with its long narrow blade nosed to a point; its jagged teeth gnawed back and forth at this, his first fib: being only a little one, an inch long.

But the next day, Hannibal couldn't resist. He insisted he'd risen before dawn, made a peanut butter and honey sandwich, and walked by himself to the pier, where the same fishboat captain had clapped him on the shoulder and invited him aboard. This time Hannibal caught a swordfish—which was even now at the taxidermist, being stuffed; the captain had promised to pay the costs, which shouldn't be over a dollar.

Despite the pain and the blood, Hannibal was enmeshed; he couldn't stop imagining fish—sole, flounder, halibut—and telling lies about them. Lies such as, 'Each is a glorious shimmering leaf plucked from the Tree of Paradise!'—his eyes shining as he babbled. He told ten lies in all, afterwards sawing away dutifully on the hoe: its handle being finally reduced to a stub, so that his grandfather, gardening, grew more and more stooped. When he finally toppled and lay still, his grandson quit lying; never again opening his mouth except to eat—though never fish.

I could go on, I could say that Hannibal became a sailor, with his dead grandfather's moustache and charm, and with his same meaty hands; but in Hannibal's case, each finger was tipped with a barbed hook, so that love was out of the question. Walking in port cities, he kept his hands thrust into his pockets unless counting out change. Only in the Chinatowns of the world did his hands with their hooks draw no comment. In fact, in San Francisco he once pursued for two blocks a petite and beautiful Oriental, her long sharp fingernails painted a blood red. But he lost her in the milling crowd and the swirl of dialects; and as he passed in front of a popular fishmarket, Hannibal found himself caught in the current and pulled through the door and inside.

The sawdust underfoot lifted in waves. Voices swelled in a high-pitched cacophony. Hannibal was pressed up against a display of red snapper, nestled on a bed of ice. Overlapped, the fish lay row upon row, like children in an orphanage sleeping on their sides but with an eye staring up, as if rudely awakened, each caught dreaming the same stunned lightbulb.

As I say, I could go on. But the fish Hannibal finally grasped to his satisfaction—a rosily-speckled brook trout that he snagged with his hands and then threw back, writhing and dangling ten silver hooks as it splashed to the water—was only this long.

Lambs

Ophelia, having peered through a telescope once,
knows the day-moon to be cold and inhuman
yet under its faded gaze continues weeping.

Having noted, Yes, how Clouds dissolve
... 'to form a *new* face, quite as handsome—and *lambs!*'
she continues weeping.

Hearing the Rain—restrained till now out of courtesy—
finally beat upon the roof and
pour from the eaves

she lifts her head: eats a cracker, some soup;

and nods, Yes, knowing Wind, as it trembles leaves
and bows limbs to the earth,
is nothing in itself, and asks nothing, even to be remembered.

Dragons

Dragons can fly, breathe fire, disappear. She-dragons are fierce to guard their young, which take five thousand years to hatch. There is room enough inside a dragon's skull for several human children to comfortably sit and peer out, taking turns at the eyes.

Dragons never tire of oiling their leathern wings, and testing the hinges. In wrath, the scales of the armour lift like whitecaps on an alpine lake. Storm appeased, the scales are lowered, to lie smooth as isinglass and reflect passing clouds.

Certain myths pursue dragons: they comb like fog through the cedars and firs, forcing the dragons to move their nests— great rusted coils of barbed wire—higher, above the tree line. The legends persist: that a dragon's saliva cures heartbreak; that their livers, sliced lengthwise, open on pearls. (If you see two dragons fighting in the air, however, expect rain.)

Archæologists refute the popular belief that from a dragon's tooth, sown, an army will spring; for they are rare, and rarely found intact; though a molar will sometimes push through the gum of an old mountain to pose as a rock, warm granite on which a hiker will stop to rest.

Few have witnessed the mating of dragons. They fly in tandem, spiralling up through the ionosphere, their scales impervious to cosmic rays. There they hover for a moment—to gaze deeply into each other's eyes, and beg the pardon of any ancestors lingering in the iris. After which they embrace, mating as they fall to earth through the seven layers of the personality.

Dik-Dik

Buff-coloured, slender and trembling, as swift in retreat as the elegant eland, the dik-dik is the smallest of antelopes, only a morsel. He boasts a flesh delicious to the carnivores of Africa and Old Europe, yet was given only one defence by the Creator: his very sweetness. When run to ground, as his heart pounds and his toothpick legs thrash the air, the dik-dik's enormous brown eyes gaze up with calm comprehension: *You must be hungry,* they say, *You must be starving.*

The attacker, abashed, loses her appetite, and begins to lick the wounds she herself has inflicted. The dik-dik, wiser, his coat moist and wavy with spit, gains his spindly legs and is allowed to wobble off.

Soon he begins to trot, his hide drying in little curls. He finds his way among the network of paths through the underbrush; pausing to nibble at a favourite flavour of leaf. The savannah is loved as a place familiar, explored; a thousand acres of flat earth, which at the edges frays into nothingness.

Off the map, mythical creatures swim-fly-gallop in the ether; they have yet to evolve, to pull themselves up onto the floating square of memory. Beyond the fringes of the known world, predators abound. Insatiable, they prowl the margins, sniffing for game which doesn't yet exist: for those animals fanciful but patient, posing under the pencil of a child whose grip chokes a sweaty stub of lead. The gentle beast holds still, allowing itself to be drawn.

And erased.

And drawn again. The hooves are wrong.

The Edwardian Elephant Seal

It is possible to picnic upon an elephant seal, spreading the red checkered cloth over the sun-warmed boulder. The china teacups rise and fall imperceptibly. Any rude noises are ignored or assigned to the smirking children.

> The head is tiny. It consists of two shut eyes embedded in the snoring granite.

The view is fine, with a tiny island to the south, and a chain of rocks leading out to it, dot dot dot, through the incoming surf. Each wave as it crashes rattles the teacups and dashes up a fine chilling spray against their faces, chins lifted to the sea breeze.

> The sea elephant, though not a shape-shifter, will also patiently allow himself to be mistaken for a rowboat—barnacled, overturned on the sand, dozing; occasionally flicking his two ridiculously tiny flippers, either side.

'Do you think it will leak?'
'Let's try it!'
The basket is packed, crumbs are brushed from laps and descent made to the sand. The children are already grunting between shouts as they crouch to right the boat. Both women get a grip by an oarlock. 'One ... Two ... *Three!*' They are going to the island.

> Left behind on the sand you will find scabs of brownish-grey fur, tiny pieces of hide shed by the elephant seals, it being the season. With fresh new coats they will mate; the males first sorting out their differences. The mature Alpha-bull boasts a huge proboscis, a cascading protuberance of flesh considered

vital to combat; an endowment which on a warm June day he waggles obscenely in front of the ladies.

Out on the island there is little room to manœuvre. Along the shore were those 'boulders,' shifting as they lolled in the sun; and now on the slope leading up to the lighthouse (its glass eye put out), hundreds of harbour seals squeal and bark: they smile up, a crowd parting like a dark, oil-slicked sea before the visitors' every step.
'Look! A volleyball net!'
The grid of string sags like a wormy flag from a pole. The seal pups crowd the court; to chase and be chased in turn by the squealing children while a thousand blinking eyes look on.
The two women are exploring the house: two-storey weatherboard with gingerbread trim, the windows long ago smashed from their sockets by incoming tides.

An Alpha-bull can swallow a seal pup whole when its mother isn't looking. The grieving parent will then follow the bull for miles through the waves, as her child is being digested.
The speed of an Alpha-bull humping towards you along the shore is due to a massive momentum as his body is lifted on flippers and thrust forward by the muscle of his tail—an appendage I forgot to mention. This forward thrust of the blubber increases exponentially over the distance you flee. The elephant seal can easily overtake a human; but is little interested.
He would rather turn in mock attack against one of his fellows, for practice. The two bulls square off, roaring. And lifting high on their flippers and waggling their 'things' in the air, they ram their chests together with a mighty *smack!* proceeding to buss

like Frenchmen back and forth, either cheek, with loud dissenting snorts.

The women have gained the second storey, their children following them up the staircase only to slide down the balustrade as the harbour seals watch from below, eyes glistening and dark. The audience grows: more seals squirm through the open doorway. They lurch on their flippers through the hall, the parlour, the kitchen of their empty playhouse—where an inch of water now skims across the floor.
Who had lived here?
'Daphne ...?' Upstairs, a bedroom door, pushed open, reveals a room bare of furniture; the roses on the wallpaper hang drooping and torn, water dripping from the petals. From across the hall a voice calls gaily, 'Come in here, Cornelia!'
And the woman obeys, gently closes the door, and crosses to another bedroom: where she presses close by her sister's side and clutches her hand as they stare down at the seal. Cornered, he blinks up at them: his body sleek, untrousered, his whiskers twitching. How could he have gotten in, *except by the second-storey window?*
Downstairs in the bathroom, seals cavort in the filling claw-footed tub; they take turns at a belly-slide along the rust which feathers towards the drain. As water continues spilling in over the sides of the tub, the seals spill out, and swim to the kitchen, their whiskered noses poking above the tide's surface. The sea is now lapping up the stairs as they swim through the parlour—where along with the children and their panicked cries they are washed out over the windowsill.

From a distance, the snorts and roars of the warring bulls assume a rusted, mechanical rhythm—as of a sump-pump, navy surplus. Here the dunes lift, and succulents take grip of the sand. Farther back on the peninsula, flowers extend yellow whiskers, and loose their mustard pungence across the bent, gently nodding grass. Birds with long expansive tails rise from the marsh trailing sharp cries against the distant industry of the bulls—*Whump! ... stut stut stut.*

Down the path amble two women in long skirts; one carries the basket, the other twirls a parasol. Their children lag behind ... and now push past; skipping towards us, towards the sea and the smell of the sea. The yellow flowers tremble on their stems, and bend, inland, hinting in that direction: *Go back.* It's just a suggestion. And premature.

For these people live here.

The land bridge will not be washed away for years yet. The caretaker's house stands newly-built on Lighthouse Point; the volleyball net eagerly awaited in the mail.

And this evening, after dark and after the children lie tucked in an upstairs bedroom, their father's light will sweep across their sleeping faces as it passes the window and swings out to sea; the beam of light stretching to the furthest sailor ... a warning blink from the past.

Cruelty to Animals

Cruel! to whip four horses to the Four Directions,
whip them until they strain at their harnesses and ... *PULL!*
the hapless criminal's torso into quarters.

Cruel to teach a dog, any dog, to bare his teeth and growl and leap at
the throat of someone he doesn't know.

Worse, to breed in cruelty, and prize it in the fighting cock,
spurring him on to damnation. All for Sport.

To blind a peregrine to all but the kill is an art, for Art's sake,
the falcon turning rhymed couplets as he wings his way back
to the poet's wrist.

And for Love's sake?

I can close a fist over my Hector's heart—knowing
that no matter how far I throw it, the beast will bring it
back, and panting, drop it at my feet.

Look! he sprawls by the hearth, eyelids closing, and sighs.
He knows I'm writing about him.

With the slightest of sounds, I can make his ears twitch;
by merely grinding the tip of the pen to
this little period . for instance

A Working Elephant

And I quote: 'Unlike other trees, palm trees do not have growth rings. Thus there is no way to determine their exact age. It is thought that some of the largest palms are as much as 250 years old ....'

The elephant, too, lives long. He is known for his patience, for his slow, swinging grace; for his sudden trumpetings of 'HALLELUJAH!' in the middle of a day's work. An elephant can uproot a palm tree with his trunk, and carry it several hundred feet before laying it down upon the others to be burned.

The question has been raised by a gentleman at the back of the room: 'Does a working elephant ever put his foot down?'

The answer is, rarely, unless to demonstrate obedience. On command, the elephant will reluctantly lower his foot to his master's head and hold it there, hold it for as long as he's told. Truly, the elephant is one of the great beasts. His spirit cannot be broken, yet he needs no yoke, he can be led on a piece of cotton string.

Not so the palm tree. There is no taming of that species, once they reach the desert. In groups of ten or twenty they'll stand shimmering in the distance, suggesting water: one's thirst only prods the mirage, keeping it on the move.

At the end of the elephant's long life, there is little left. The tusks are sawn into lengths of ivory; the hide stretched over drums; the penis dried and weighed.

As for that Foot, you might notice it in the hall as you depart into the rainy streets. It's right by the door: a grey and toenailed elephant's foot, hollowed out. And don't forget your umbrella.

The Cow

'Playing House' it is called, and learned as a child. With a stick, the girl draws a square in the dirt. Then with pebbles she divides kitchen from living room; living room from where they'll sleep—unless the baby cries, and until the Daddy goes to work.

'Remember, we've sold the Cow,' she instructs the boy, who shrugs.

'And we're very poor.'

'Okay.'

But already he's walked through a wall; and now wanders off with his slingshot.

Boys will do this. They forget where they live. And if they do come back, they forget which-room-is-which; they forget the name of the baby; they don't recognize ... what these buttons are, that they're eating.

Women

High-strung, they're always transporting
this & that: the thorax of a compatriot
or some useful bit of fluff, or what looks like a grain
of cooked rice, but proves to be the future.

And lighter stuff, a man, if it so amuses. A current of
black, narrow-waisted notes might pulse through the
mind of a genius like Bach as a cantata

and then refuse, veer off the page to
vagaries.

Though they'll never cross synapse to neuron for a man who
doesn't love women in all their ways; forgetting things
and doubling back, for instance,
or the instinct to seize a man's tiniest fault
    and hold it aloft between pincers.

Worm

Dressed for tennis, the Lessee paces the hall. Along the windowsill, the house plants in his keeping pant with thirst; they lean in unison towards the scrap of paper in his hand, thinking it their watering schedule. He ignores them; continues talking into the telephone, his profile beaked and plumed.

'Sweetie, I'm going to hang up, this is getting us nowhere.' He stares down at his foot, where the phone cord lies coiled in a circle, an innocuous white lasso.

'... Look, it doesn't mean *anything*.'

Or it could be one of the long white intestinal worms diagnosed by that quack Iridologist: something to do with lesions in the iris. He leans forward into the hall mirror ...

'Alright, I'll call you tomorrow. Yes. *Yes,* I promise!'

Gazing into his reflection, he can almost feel them: swimming in the watery blue of his pupils. *Hiding out in the whites.*

Two Birds, One Stone

I

When a man recounts a nightmare from his childhood, over a litre of wine and the waxy breath of a shared candle, the woman listening will give her full attention to the story: it might prove the key to the man's affections; a key she will then throw away, or keep in a safe place for later use.

'I ran, I stumbled across the prairie, pursued by a great huge bird. I could hear its wings thrashing the air overhead as it readied to swoop down ... and then I woke.'

His listener leaned forward: *'How* big?'

'Well, big enough to carry off a buffalo for a snack!' When he smiled the man looked younger. His thick black brows fronted a forehead which slanted steeply back. He was watching for her reaction.

Not that he ever turned to look behind him as he ran. In the Ukraine where he was born, such dreams as his could sink their talons in and carry a young victim great distances, over hectares of wheat, before losing grip of a boy's pyjamas. Each time, he woke from the nightmare soaked with sweat, staring up into the dark. He was twelve. He resolved, *Never again.*

'The following night I dreamt that I slipped from my bed and crept out into the moonlight. On a distant ridge I found the nest of the bird. The nest was huge, and inside lay a single egg. I picked up a large stone, and held it high over my head—and smashed it down.'

'Oh.'

The corners of his mouth turned up—the mischievous grin of a twelve-year-old. 'The next night when I found myself running through waist-high wheat with the bird chasing after me, I suddenly remembered about the egg. I stopped. And as I turned around to finally face my nemesis, it softly settled upon my shoulder with a rustle of feathers, a kind of ... sigh. Into my ear it murmured, "I understand."'

'But you'd smashed its only egg!'

'Yes, I know. It was a mess.' From staring at the candle he looked up with a rueful smile. 'And yet all these years, that's all the bird has ever said to me, no matter what trouble I get myself into. Just, "I understand."'

(When anyone—man or woman—confesses to a deed which is only human, there is usually a vital detail left unspoken, a crumb brushed off in the telling. Only in going back over the story does one notice it, lying there in plain sight.)

The two sat in silence. The candle flame did a jig in the soft draft.

The good fellow grew expansive, tipping back in his chair. 'I've been telling people for years about my bird,' he confessed, 'but you're the first person who could imagine it.'

And indeed, they were now three at table, for the woman was staring across at the man's left shoulder, at the occupant perched there. 'How wonderful ...' She spoke wistfully, her eyes shining in the candlelight.

'What?'

By this time the litre of house wine was emptied, and a shift was about to occur in the conversation.

'To be understood, no matter what ...'

And then it happened, the words flew from his lips as of their own accord—'You can have my bird!'

She stiffened—'But what will you do without it?!'— as the calm, feathered presence alighted on her shoulder.

'I'll be fine.' He grinned. 'Something else will come along.' He seemed pleased with himself, even relieved.

The stale crumb mentioned previously, the one brushed off, is similar in function to the pea which irritated a certain princess to distraction: being a small, round, hard fact, on which a romance might pivot. The fact being: the egg this man had smashed as a boy had been ready, any moment, to hatch.

The woman suspects as much. Or rather, suspects there is something that her new lover would rather forget, that he refuses to admit to memory. Something he'd done a long time ago; a petty sin he committed which he still prefers to ignore, and which thus looms larger than a boulder in his soul.

Now, no one likes to be reminded of what they pretend they don't know. And when eventually she calls him to task in a rising voice, his own voice booms back harsh with anger:

'I never asked you to come chasing after me!'

It's almost midnight. Quarrelling, the couple walks down a road flanked either side with tall poplars. Their loud voices carry across the moonlit fields as they near a farmhouse—set back from the road by a hundred yards. Lights still shine from the kitchen's bay window. A dog begins to bark, his long chain rattles and then chokes taut as he strains forward—barking, barking at the shadowed figures passing between the poplars.

'Hector, hush!' comes the sharp instruction from the porch of the farmhouse, then the bang of a screen door.

For a moment the dog obeys, he allows slack to gather and droop in his chain.

And then it pulls at him again—the presence of a fellow creature out there on the road: one he can sense but not see, smell but not hear. Again he runs to the length of his chain and, throwing himself at the taunting presence, he ravishes the night with his hoarse shouts.

The man strides on ahead down the road, hunch-shouldered, hands thrust into his pockets. His pursuer lags behind, overtaken by shivers; she clutches her arms, she's forgotten her coat. To the man's broad back she blurts out ... well, she blurts out another wild accusation, another reproach wide of the mark. And then halts in the middle of the road. 'I ... didn't mean to say that,' her voice suddenly meek. And then, 'But it's true!'

With his back to her the man strides on ahead; striding upon the shadows which the poplars cast down across the road, as before a King of Creation. He draws his shoulders around his neck, like a thick muscular cowl. 'I don't care what you do with it!' he shouts back over his shoulder, in answer to the woman's question.

Behind him, she hesitates, standing in the middle of the road. Tears of frustration fill her eyes, and anger at these same tears provokes her to again wail forth her question—*'What am I going to do with this bird?!'*

The attendant poplars stand neutral and aloof.

The dog continues his frenzied barking as the woman hurries to catch up. She breaks into a trot: the feathery mass of the bird riding effortlessly upon her shoulder as she pursues the argument.

II

Cozy inside the lit bay window of the farmhouse, the black raven is busy within his cardboard box. From the kitchen ceiling a single bald lightbulb sheds its glare. The bird prefers this to the dark; for when the kitchen is consigned to the blackness appropriate to sleep, he cries continuously in a most piteous croak, as if reliving a familiar nightmare. But with the bulb left harshly burning, like a false sun, all in the house can rest; the silence being broken only when Hector barks at one of his many phantoms, projected from an unquiet conscience.

The raven is gnawing the cardboard box that squares his world. The box is a fresh one brought home from the grocer's, and the bird is altering it to fit. His smooth black head now appears above the top of the carton: he has gnawed out a view—of the moonlit yard and the distant poplars.

The dog Hector has turned from his barking; his chain now

drags behind him in defeat.

The raven also: dragging a maimed wing across the newsprint lining his box. The news-of-the-day has been changed regularly for him these nineteen years. He is, in fact, a honeymoon memento, found on a grassy knoll where the newlyweds had gone to lie. The fledgling—still wet as he struggled through the grass—was a pitiful sight. One wing would never be more than a feathered crutch. *Who had done this?*

Raven as pet, then: fed a joint from the soup to worry for the week; and tidbits of digestive cookie, for which he cocks his small black head, still wary. For the moment, half-past midnight under the sunny glare of the lightbulb, he paces his box. Hunch-shouldered, he inspects a freshly soiled headline beneath his claws.

And then spies something—in plain sight. A neglected crumb.

As for this dry morsel, I suspect it's what that woman—shivering and still quarrelling out on the road—is trying to put her finger on.

And could we but admit a raven his memories—of exploding eggshell lodging like shrapnel in his flesh, and a large cold stone smashing down in place of his mother, flown—we could say, *Wait! That's the evidence! That's what the woman is trying to get at!*

As things are ... the raven pecks, lifts the crumb in his black beak, tips back his head, and swallows.

Moth

                                                                                            up.
                                                                         flutters
From the sweep of the broom a dead moth

        Some moths have great downy eyes
        on their wings; eyes
        wise, wide open, gazing at you
        as the moth sleeps.

                        Moths keep different hours
                        than ours.

To catch a moth while
reading in bed at night

simply hold up your fist and relax the fingers
to the shape of a lightbulb:

the moth will flutter in.

                        Switch off the lamp,
                        a busy fly falls silent.

                        while a moth in the dark

                        finds your face,
                        in case you were sleeping.

Men

The variety in which the flesh clings to the stone
was never my mother's favourite
nor is it mine: less sweet, less shaggy with juice
    (they require a knife)
than if you wait

till later in the season, for the other kind to ripen
and fall into your lap,
fall open between your thumbs
and run down your chin and between your breasts.

These also dry best.

Spider Web

No one knows why a snake, slithering through grass, will refuse to cross a spider's web.

A strand of web has the tensile strength of a line of music.

I have seen webs thirty feet long, floating high above the lake and heading south.

Imagine returning to your web just as the moon is freeing itself.

A web of lies can be spun from a single kiss.

In France, black cobwebs droop heavy with soot from the vaulted ceiling of a convent. Black mediæval chains. Nothing like the starched white wings the nuns wear to your face.

From his cheek, I pluck a small black spider. He says it was only one kiss.

The Fox, the Rabbit, the Duck

The life of the shadow puppet is brief. Made of fingers—and cast on the bedroom wall by children listening while their parents make love—the Fox can drop his jaw, he can talk. But only in a whisper. He is saying to the Rabbit, *I am going to eat you up.*

To that, the Rabbit can only wriggle her long, knuckled ears; or choose to loom larger on the wall, her black shadow muffling that of the Fox.

And here comes the Duck, *Quack quack.* He is looking for his mother. *Are you my mother?* he asks the Rabbit. They kiss. They knock their heads together. A thin shuddering cry issues through the wall.

Lepus the Hare

When the pups are grown and scattered and wary, the coyote will get more rest. She will sleep during the day. For now, she leaves the pups only at night—in order to carry, from horizon to horizon, the constellation Lepus upon her back.

All night long, the Hare, glittering and pure and eternal, travels on the back of its dearest enemy and arouses no lust. Not once does the coyote turn her head. Steadily she trots through the scrub of the desert; while the eight stars of Lepus cling to the fur of her withers like burrs caught fast. Only when the sky begins to lighten does the coyote slow her pace, relieved of her burden as the stars fade to the horizon.

She doubles back. Now she is free to hunt. With dawn, the desert air pearls with moisture, however brief. Myriad scents loose themselves to the coming warmth. And whereas through the night, clear cold thinking was possible, black and white—with dawn comes Creation: the starry archetype of Lepus fills in with sweet, plump flesh.

The coyote catches a whiff. Her nostrils quiver. And instead of the straight, steady lope of the night across the desert, she twists and turns through the sagebrush after the leaping, terrified hare.

She drops the limp creature at the mouth of the den, the smell of blood rousing the pups.

No wonder the constellations travel only by night,
lest they be devoured.

The Crab of Logic

Little in nature follows a straight path; usually the wandering is at will through the landscape. It takes years for a path to feel its way among trees; to edge down a slope. The animals then take it for granted: the game trail was always like this, smelling of their shed fur and droppings.

Creeks as well follow the path of least resistance. A zig-zag between stones, left, right, a headlong plunge into foam and on down ... until the valley is reached. Here, the river elbows wider curves, as it slows and meanders and matures. There is no sense in hurrying.

The Buddha knew this. To simply be on a path, to take off your shoes and socks and walk barefoot is to be alive on this earth and no other. The foot shapes itself over stick and stone. The internal organs are thus stimulated. The flame of spontaneous will dances up and down the spine of the child. He breathes in the piney air as he walks along the path to catch the schoolbus.

Earlier that morning he'd obeyed his mother's command to 'hold still'—as she steadied his head, and combed his damp brown hair forward.

'Why must I go to school?'

At school, with their rulers, the children are drawing connections between the stars. In the sky are many constellations; the one being studied today is Cancer, the crab. The crab is known for its eccentric, sideways pattern of locomotion.

'But why must I?'

'Hush.' His mother's face is close above his own, her breath warm upon his brow as she cups his chin.

At the crown of his head, he feels the end-tooth of the comb dig gently into his skull. His mother traces a dead-straight part; then combs his hair to one side, and the other.

And if the child is a girl?

You sit behind her, on a stool. With the comb centred at her widow's peak, you draw the comb towards you, up over the crown of her head; keeping a steady hand as you draw the comb on down to the nape of her neck. Then, taking up the brush, you gather half of her hair into your fist and brush it; brush it as she asks her questions. To braid, you divide the hank into three strands, and fold them in upon each other as you work your way down the braid; and stretch a red rubber band around the stub.

Then the other side. Brushing. Plaiting the gathered strands into a smooth rope, down and down as it dwindles in your fingers; ending in another stub; another red rubber band. And a tug to the bell of her head: *There, you're done.*

And then she's gone, out the door.

What stays with you is the parting at the back of your daughter's head, dividing her braids; a line of white, waxy scalp which you gently furrowed and revealed; and which, except with a mirror held awkwardly, she can't see.

The Wrung Neck of a Swan

In England, only the fellows of St. John's College, Cambridge, have the right to kill a swan. This is an ancient privilege, and must be exercised once a year, or be forfeited. Once a year, a swan must be caught; one of the fellows must wrap his arms around her breast and pin the panicked wings and hold the creature trembling against his own beating heart.

When the swan has been stuffed and roasted, she is lifted on her silver platter, and carried shoulder-high into the dining hall. Long, elegant neck stiffly arched, she sails in for the Feast of the Swan with head bowed, as if concerned for the eggs nestled round her on the platter.

The cooked flesh is black, strangely sweet, difficult to chew. And known to provoke dreams of a disturbing nature.

One of the fellows lays down his napkin. He has only picked with his fork at the meat; and now excuses himself—to walk along the river's tarry lights.

Swans glide over the black water. On the bank, a lamppost bows its head. The River Cam flows on past, under tremulous glories, cast on its surface.

In the dream, he's approaching the cottage where his mother lives alone. The eaves sag with years of bougainvillæa.

He's about to knock, he's raised his fist ... when the door opens and his uncles brush past. They've hefted the mortgage to their shoulders, and carry it now down the steps and out the gate.

Her heart.

'You broke your mother's heart,' one of the uncles calls back over his shoulder, not unkindly, but in a flat voice.

And he's left alone on the porch, with its rotting floorboards.

He ventures in; into the darkened kitchen and his mother's bruised scent.

And there's his old thirst in its jar on the counter!

He clutches the wrung neck of his gift—the stem of a popular song.

His mother had been fine. She'd been ironing; and was buttoning a blouse on its hanger—squeezing the last button through a tiny stitched hole—when the breast pocket swung open.

The Great Blue Heron

Bravo! A great blue heron has swooped down. She stalked across the lawn, and is now plucking goldfish from the pool—to swallow whole their delicious struggles.

I prefer to rise early, before my host, and before the cloud hovering low over the lake can disperse. At this hour, from the garden, I can gaze down upon the cloud's white woolly back—and think of England's grazing flocks.

As for the Rockies: the mountains here censor any view but of themselves. I will grant the stars over Canada their tiresome brilliance, but wilderness, wilderness—why so many trees? A miracle, that the heron spied this tonsured patch on which to alight.

And look how she stalks about the garden! Granted, her neck is overlong. She stands on one leg—yet is she mocked as an eccentric? Because she is tall, does one call her grace 'awkward'? It seems that word hasn't yet reached her, of her imminent extinction. *'Oblivion has claimed the Sitwells'?* I agree with you, Osbert, we shall bring suit—much as I would prefer to ignore the grubbing robins with their worms.

Look how she stands, one claw lifted in disdain. O, I wish you could see her. Wind ruffles her pale blue feathers. Always at this hour, as the sun attempts to rise over the thick-headed mountains, a breeze stirs. My papers get blown about. Beside my camp desk, a full-grown *Cranbee-cordata* sways on her stalk. A veritable giantess, with huge flapping leaves—and all from a single cutting, smuggled out through the gate at Kew Gardens in a handkerchief.

And now she reigns in this outpost. Turbaned with a single splendiferous bloom, she towers above the lesser flowers as I attempt to scribble, despite the wind, this letter to my dear, dear brothers ...

Your loving Edith
6 July 1940

Intelligence in the Kingdom

> *0, full of Scorpions is my Minde*
> Shakespeare

I

In the male TURKEY is displayed an intelligence rarely seen in the animal kingdom. Freed of the cranium, the cerebrum of a Tom cascades fold upon fold over the brow, in shades of pale blue and rose, with a long ooze of medulla dangling down over the beak.

You can pet him, he will let you. He will turn the other cheek, presenting a walleye in profile, and a tiny ear which is merely a hole; one can poke a sharpened pencil through and out the other side.

II

When constrained within a skull, the brain is consistently colourless and compact—no bigger than a walnut in which case a SQUIRREL. In this case, the two hemispheres press between them a plain brown membrane: when the nut is cracked and the two halves pried apart, this brown scrap of paper flutters out, blank on either side. The brain is a mystery.

III

Sometimes a single brain is divided up among the members of a community, as with BEES. All cells firing simultaneously, busy, busy.

The single bee—however far from the hive—doesn't think for himself. So if stung when you were only trying to help, don't ask why. The drone doesn't know. (The sting of a HORNET is more intentional, more likely to be poisoned with a gleam of free will.)

IV

The HUMAN brain is another animal altogether.

Consider the brain of a common foot soldier. A chain of scorpions lowers itself slowly and carefully from the ceiling of the tent. Each scorpion in turn stings the soldier below who lies sleeping on his cot. In his ensuing delirium, the poor fellow becomes convinced he's to blame. *Yes, yes I am! Nature is impartial! It's my own fault for being here in the first place! I deserve it, I deserve to die!*

This is called introjection: the brain stinging itself.

An Elk, Still Thinking

In the silence, a single leaf, then another, and then a flutter of leaves falls with the patter of brief rain. Yet the morning sky remains clear; a clear blue, above the blue of the lake. The elk, having drunk his fill, lifts his head at the sound of a snapping twig.

Think of it: from your temples issues a slow eruption of bone, like calcified thought, branching into the ether.

The elk, still thinking, holds his pose: antlers stretching wide to embrace all questions. An impressive sight, when he emerged from the woods, to pick his way down the game trail to the lake for a drink.

Champagne came to mind: eight full glasses balanced on one set of points, and eight on the other set. Below was the steep bank. The elk dug his front hooves into the dirt, and, leaning back on his haunches, eased himself down with short, careful steps. All the while, he balanced on his head that great mossy rack, without spilling a drop.

One drink leads to another.

And to the morning after. Oh, to lift the racking throb at the temples into the air, and there carry it about, the branching capillaries cooled by a breeze. Catching sight of these raw, exposed nerves, even strangers would observe that I have a headache, and lower their voices to the stillness of the Indian summer.

And then I could shed them, I could rub my head against a tree.

Wild Turkey

When the cavities have been filled with the stuffing of your choice, stitch the neck shut, and the rump. The wings must lie closely tucked at the sides of the bird. The estimated cooking time for a turkey is twenty minutes to the pound.

While the turkey cooks *(and is basted every half hour or so)*, Uncle Bill eases the phonograph needle into the groove of a waltz. Wild Turkey on his breath, he stands waiting, arms outstretched for his young niece. He wears brown slacks, a relaxed golf sweater, and on his feet, polished brown wingtips.

She crosses the room in her ankle socks. As instructed, she steps up onto her uncle's shoes, and circles her arms up around his waist. Her toes clutch at his laces for a grip.

Ready?

The oven door is opened with a mitt, the syringe is nosed under the turkey and the juices sucked up—to be squirted over the nicely browning breast.

One-two-three, one-two-three, Uncle Bill begins to waltz her across the floor. Her knees buckle as her stockinged feet are lifted with her Uncle's every step—Light on your feet, light!

One-two-three, one-two-three, he glides her backwards in time to the music as her feet lift by no effort of their own, he is teaching her to dance like an angel.

Then comes a pause between waltzes. She holds on as he leans sideways to change the record. The soles of her feet clutch his insteps. For what seems a very long time, she stares at her uncle's leather belt, at the little brass tongue, poking through a hole. For what seems like a vast mindless stretch of time, the afternoon's full white span, unclipped, spreading wingtip to wingtip ….

Baste.

Another Beast

Fire, of all the beasts, has not evolved. There's been no need, fire is supremely flexible, resilient. It worms its way into the least likely of objects. Take stones: two rubbed together will emit sparks. Even a pig's eyes burn with the Wisdom of the Serpent.

Ubiquitous, indiscriminate, fire remains pure, and leaves no aftertaste. Fire-eaters soon lose their appetite for anything less. The retired fireman will lean back in his La-Z-Boy, strike a match, and stare with nostalgia at the orange and blue flame.

A pyromaniac will gladly accept credit for any fire raging the neighbourhood—face flushed and shining in the light. Greeted by a conflagration, some people run away, or run in circles; others rush *towards* a fire and throw their coats over it. A fire is always warm, on the coldest winter afternoon. And patient, when coiled upon itself, smouldering. A mere ember of desire, lying long among the summer grass, can flare with a breeze if slowly, assiduously stroked.

But that's another afternoon, and another beast.

Polite to Bees

Even as she wakes she is being lowered into the tub by the hovering bees, a tub filled with honey.

Honey gloriously warm, like sunlight through her eyelids. Honey slow to close around her nakedness, and seal her limbs from any act of will.

She opens her eyes, or tries to.

Immersed, neck to toe, with effort she lifts one arm; lifts a curtain of honey, a sheer wing—which soon tatters, tearing holes in itself, the remnants dripping from her arm.

She lifts her other arm, lifts another wing of honey, as if she might fly, might try—without giving offence—to get up.

Bats

Trapped in a man's brain, a chronic black thought will continue to circle, emitting shrill cries which echo within his skull. Sometimes the man will shout. He'll clench his fists and punch an exit through a door, or through the wall, in order to free the terrified creature.

The man then steps out into the night—to walk, and not think. Smoking, he draws in lungfuls; and exhales, calmed by the stars' precise science.

When from the lawn he sees the bedside lamp blink out, he goes in, stubbing his cigarette before mounting the steps. The battered screen door sighs and clicks behind him. In the bedroom he opens the window—a mistake. He's of the fresh-air school, while his wife prefers the window closed. He slips his chilled bare body under the covers, and against her warmth. They both pretend she is asleep.

In the morning she closes the window her husband once again opened. But she's too late. That evening, during the six o'clock news, a bat drops from a rafter and thuds to the carpet.

While she screams, her husband rises slowly and deliberately from his chair. Kneeling down, he turns the bat over, and stretches out its wings, gently, with his fingers.

Stunned from its fall, the bat lies with its eyes pinched shut. Its slack mouth bares tiny pointed teeth. The wings, forcibly extended, want only to fold shut; fold against the puny chest.

The man holds them open. He examines the creature intently—as if it had just fallen from the roof of his brain; from a ceiling crowded black with bats just like this one, barely hanging on.

Man-Eating Tigers

'Most suspicious was when you'd be on patrol in the jungle and you'd come upon a big grey boulder—plunk in the middle of a clearing. Its surface would be too clean, no overgrowth of moss or vines. Right away, your hair would stand on end.

'I'd seen boulders like these Stateside, at the San Diego Zoo. Huge fake boulders we'd be left staring at while the tigers were being fed. They'd be pacing pacing, never looking at you. Then a small door low in the corner of their grotto would slide up: instantly the tigers veered, bounded towards that little door and disappeared into their hunger. And we'd be left with the boulders.

'I wanted to show them to my wife. So on the day of her arrival in the States, I drove her from the airport straight to the Zoo. She wouldn't take my word for it, she insisted, "Any tiger could leap that moat and be at our throats—those aren't real tigers." She said their stripes were painted on.

'The most magnificent boulders I've ever come across are right here on the Coast Range. When I first came home from 'Nam I used to hike a lot. And the underbrush grows so thick and lush—I had to fight my way through it. Well, I was climbing, I looked up—and there was this boulder. A man-eater. It rose up, perfectly smooth and grey, no plant-life could get a grip, not even lichen.

'I sat down—right here, at your feet. I closed my eyes, I forced my mind to pierce the boulder, to penetrate into its hollow core. I must have blacked out. When I came to, the sun was down, but the boulder remained.

'So I built this house around it, with room enough down here at the base for my easel, a hotplate, our cot. You can't imagine what it's like to live with a boulder, with its presence. I've heard guys say that if you look into the eyes of a big cat in the jungle—straight into those yellow slits—you finally comprehend the depth of God's indifference, His greatness. That's what it's like when you live with one of these: you start to feel them.

'Yeah, put your hand on it. Try it. Go on, it won't bite.

'Only thing is, the boulder and my wife don't get along. She complains it takes up all the room, she wants what she calls a 'real' kitchen, so she can be a real American wife.

'And she's always cold. I tell her, "It's the change of climate, Kim." But no, she claims the boulder steals the heat.'

Scottie Dogs

'They came in pairs, one Scottie black, the other white, and both embedded with magnets. They were very tiny, not even an inch high, and made of metal. The set was my favourite toy. I'd forgotten all about its existence—until reminded the other day by a pair of Scotch terriers, one black, one white, trotting along the cliff by the sea. I always spend several hours of the afternoon sitting on my park bench, but I'd never seen these two before.

'Free of their leashes, the Scotties followed one after the other along the path, their owner nowhere in sight. Nearing my bench, the black Scottie paused, lifted a hind leg, and signed a bush; then he crossed to sniff at the tip of my cane.

'And here came the other Scottie, with a pause at the same bush and a brief squat, before crossing to my bench like a white *déjà vu*. All the while, she kept an eye on the black Scottie who was now trotting off.

'And so she followed.

'It was as if a little magnet in the white Scottie pulled her along, and she couldn't have said why. And just as surely as she followed, the black Scottie and his magnet appeared to be urged on from behind, as by some unseen force, propelling him forward. My own husband was often gone from the house. He would say to me ... such and such, some pale excuse. I would follow him to the door, and sometimes as far as the gate. Once I took a cab, and followed at a discreet distance until I saw that he was just walking.

'It was very simple, how the magnets worked in the tiny metal Scotties of my childhood. If I squared the Scotties off, face to face, and slowly brought them together across the tabletop, I soon felt a strange pull between them, closer and closer, until ... *Snap!* I had to pry them apart.

'Tail to tail, it was the opposite case, their magnetic fields repulsed, I had to use force. Gentle force, pushing them together against their resistance.

'A third dynamic was possible if I lined them up, both faced in the same direction. Without even touching, and following at just the right distance, the Scottie in the rear could steer the one in the lead; steer him this way and that, here and there, clear across the table, and over the edge.

'Like those immigrant couples from India who cross our streets: the wife, wrapped in her sari, follows five paces back from her husband; and yet he knows she is there, he doesn't have to look, he can feel her. Otherwise he couldn't go on, there would be no reason to put one foot in front of the other—as he does, seemingly oblivious to being dutifully followed, propelled; a man of the world, needing no one.'

The Albino Parrot

'Show him in.'

Madame Rosenthal remains seated on the white sofa. She arranges the folds of her long white dress. As the young journalist enters the parlour, she pats her powdered coiffure with a withered but still elegant hand. She must have been very beautiful once.

'I know what you're thinking.'

'What is that, Ma'am?' he asks, hat in hand, as she indicates with an impatient wave: he's to sit on the white sofa opposite.

'You're thinking of how to get your story. That's all that concerns you.'

'On the contrary ...' Ducking his head, he sips from the glass of milk set before him by an aproned maid. Next he must attend to the plate of iced cakes. All the while he endures the dowager's clouded stare.

'My son had your voice. High, and guarded. And yes, the same manner of never answering me square on.'

'Madame, I am sorry about your son.'

At that she stiffens. And begins twisting one of the rings on her hand, a large blind moonstone. 'Don't you think it strange, that a grown man would leave ...'—and here she gestures, *all this*—'to paddle up a river in the jungle?'

Yes mama.

The journalist gives a start, glancing over his shoulder.

'You're puzzled.' She smooths the white linen of her skirts: 'You wonder that I'm not dressed in mourning, in black.'

'No! I assure you, I make no judgement.'

'Of course you do. But you see, my son won't let me grieve.' Her head turns on her long alabaster neck, offering him her profile as she calls across the room: 'Will you, darling.'

Yes mama, comes the muffled squawk.

The young man blanches.

Across the room stands the source of that dry, mechanical

reply: a tall birdcage, to judge from the vertical ribs which bulge through a draped white sheet.

'They say my son drowned ...' Chin still lifted and turned, Madame Rosenthal continues to direct her remarks towards the draped cage. 'Or that he was taken captive—by this tribe or that tribe. But I don't believe that he is dead.' And here her glare swivels to the sofa opposite and bores through her young guest: 'Do you?'

He gulps. Forced to meet her filmy, cataracted eyes with their white lashes, he feels faint, slightly nauseous. 'Well, I ...'

Yes mama, parrots a scratchy reply.

'Come ...' Madame R. gathers her skirts and rises, not without grace, from the white sofa. 'Come, you must meet him.' With measured steps she crosses the white parlour—white carpet, white walls, the white brocade drapes drawn closed; 'He arrived in a crate from the Amazon, on the same day I received the news ... the *rumours*, concerning my son.'

She pauses beside the tall, shrouded cage, as if overcome by the effort of a few steps. 'He's all I have left,' she intones, as her pale, elegant hand reaches up to remove the sheet: 'The only colour in my life.'

At this point, the author pauses. He sits hunched at his desk, the gas lamp flickering. Then Poe dips the pen into the ink. In a last-minute twist, he's decided that the parrot—a fine specimen, healthy, sure to live long; and intelligent, a perfect mimic, sent in good faith by a loyal and obedient son—the parrot shall arrive with a gene gone missing.

Red Flyer

The lizard is unusually fickle. She likes red, but as she crawls across the brick floor and confronts the pretty stripes of the rug, she turns purple and blue and purple in rapid succession till she reaches the fringe. Then she shimmies up the doorjamb—an easy green. She means to hide, she wants to surprise Suzanna.

And when the girl walks in with an empty basket from hanging up the clothes, the now-green lizard hurls herself into the nest of auburn hair passing below, and prepares for the ride. Her claws grip Suzanna's scalp as the girl runs screaming through the yard to her mother-in-law's house. By this time the lizard has adopted the new shade of red.

Before the dye can set, the lizard is brutally uprooted and flung through the air amid curses and shouts. She lands on the road with a thud; stunned; paling to a dusty brown as the chickens peck about.

From above, a shovel blade slices down.

The lizard finds herself cut in two. Beige and dozy, she waddles away, leaving her tail in the road. She climbs up the tongue of a little red wagon, overturned: and basks on the hot metal.

Not one thought does she give to her severed tail, which lies in the dust of the road and will soon be run over by a scooter.

Not one thought; for she still has her tail's phantom limb. In place of the old tail, it has loyally followed its lizard up the handle of the wagon; and is now filling in with flesh to match. It's a slow, cold-blooded process. As for the lizard, she is daintily snoring on the upturned belly of the *Red Flyer* abandoned by a former child.

Here we leave them, wagon and lizard, both rusting nicely.

Animals Lower Down in the Conversation

Four-thirty, closing time at the San Francisco Zoo, and the only animals allowed to go home are pushing through the squeaking turnstile. The March air smells of salt from the nearby sea. The wide walkways curving among the pens and cages are mostly deserted.

A few stragglers are taking a last look. Four teens lean against the black iron railing which surrounds a moat, which in turn surrounds a concrete island: barren of even the single palm tree allotted in the comics.

An orang-outang sits marooned. She is lifting and lowering her behind. Now she walks on her callused black knuckles to the edge of her island. Stretching out her palm, she not so much begs, as encourages onlookers to degrade themselves into tossing bits of foodstuff across the dry moat. The four teens in black leather jackets comply, laughing.

Soon she turns her back to us, while still perched at the edge. Shit is exuding from her rump, and she reaches around and grasps the turd, slowly forthcoming, in her hand. She brings the item around, brings it up to her nose, studies it; everything in her casual yet deliberate manner conveys the impression that next she will turn and fling it across the moat at her audience.

The giraffe's droppings are dainty and round; a sudden shower thudding to the dirt from a great height. Stretching the imagination even higher is her neck, as she moves with lanky nonchalance around the pen. From her brow rise two stubs of horn, two teetering stacks of copper pennies. These she balances as she chews her cud, and blinks, batting her lashes. Surely her breath is sweet. Now she ambles on her stilts to the pond, and tilts the 23rd floor of a Cairo skyscraper down to the water for a lengthy sip. Her tail swishes, a fancy riding crop, Moroccan leather. And here falls another shower of droppings—dark sweetmeats, dates.

The lions have begun their nap-time routine of roaring back and forth; huge vagrant roars, tousled and yawning roars which deafen as they echo against the boulders of the grotto and roll out across the Zoo. The big cats lie stretched on their sides, lazy amid fresh, impressive piles of feces—deposited here and there on the otherwise bare, swept concrete.

The gulls alighting on Monkey Island strut among their own white guano and peanut shells. The Island rises in tiers like a wedding cake overrun with monkeys of all kinds.

On the lowest tier, nearest the water, a mother and father spider monkey keep pace while the baby explores. The infant moves cautiously, on spindly black limbs. His long black tail curves up in a hook, posing a question mark wherever he goes. He doesn't go far without his parents. The three keep in constant touch—except when the infant forgets himself and lopes ahead to claim a gum wrapper.

His father strolls behind on all fours.

But what is this? The infant spider monkey pauses, while a rush of wings gives the signal: the gulls have lifted, and now wheel; with cries joyfully profane they circle Monkey Island.

The little monkey extends a tiny finger, and dips the tip into a fresh white blob, fallen from the sky. *What is this? Something to eat?*

His mother nears, moving on all fours, tail upcurved. Overtaken, he hops obediently to her back; riding low, his tail winding up around hers, a black tendril twining up around the larger question.

A Common Parasite

The phobia is a common parasite. In essence a suffix, a little tail or flagellum, the phobia attaches itself to a wide variety of hosts. Thus dawn, women, vacuum cleaners, comets, drawbridges—all have a following.*

There are those who pooh-pooh the phobia, and claim to fear nothing but fear itself (Phobo-phobics). More commonly, we fear *something.* Blake feared symmetry. And we usually fear more than one thing at a time. Many a Claustro-phobic has wriggled out of a tight spot, scraping elbows and shins, only to confront Agora-phobia—fear of the open sky.

Only the snake has no fear: would hardly notice a phobia, way back there, hanging on. Of course, the more effort spent to rid oneself of a phobia, the more tenaciously it clings. And no use trying to help someone else with a phobia—by giving a good sharp yank, or carefully burning it off with a hot needle or a lit cigarette. The best tack, if you suspect you're being followed, is to brush it off as nothing. Keep walking. Don't look back, don't give a phobia the satisfaction.

Tremo-phobics, Mania-phobics, Parasito-phobics, Papa-phobics (imagine, fearing the Pope!), Auro-phobics, Dora-phobics—I fear the list is too long to enumerate. Except to mention that some sillies—Logo-phobics—fear *words.*

Conversely, there's a word, one of my favourites, which fears being trapped half-formed in a pedant's brain. One moment, it's just on the tip of my tongue ... *Ahhh!* The word is Bromidrosi-phobia: fear of bad breath.

---

*Eoso-phobia, Gyne-phobia, Mechanophobic-acoustico-phobia, Cometo-phobia, Gephyro-phobia

Right Front

'Breakfast was running smoothly, and I turned to the stove with a bowl of eggs—beaten to a froth along with some chopped green onion, grated cheese, a pinch of basil. I reached down to twist on the knob for RIGHT FRONT ...'

'She forgot—that burner doesn't work, I have to fix it. The knob is in my shop.'

'... A grey conical head protuded, a mouse with his hair slicked back.'

'Right here, peering out from this dime-size hole—it won't even take my finger.'

'His whiskers measured his error. He was stuck.'

'The little guy didn't flinch when she screamed.'

'You're the one who screamed, Frank.'

'Whoever. But the mouse was dead.'

'I wasn't sure, I waved the spatula in front of his glittering stare ....'

'I figure he died of fright. He was in there chewing on crumbs, she banged the frying pan down, and he saw that little circle of light and made a run for it.'

'... Not a bright idea.'

'He was stuck good and tight. I tried nudging him back with the Want Ads.'

'Frank brought me the pliers. I pried the burner up, and reached in and pinched his grey little tail, among all those wires.'

'You could have been electrocuted.'

'Frank turned off the breaker, I'm always forgetting things like that. But here's the interesting question: Why did the mouse forget himself? Did he really think he could fit through that tiny hole and escape? Or in his panic, did his judgement short-circuit, did he simply forget he had a body?'

'He was good and fat. It took a couple of tugs with the pliers before she lifted him out, hanging upside down by his tail. I felt terrible.'

'Or did he truly think for a split second that he *was* his head, and since his head could surely slip through—*Cogito, ergo sum* ...'

'You caught him by surprise, Sweetie.'

'... An assumption which leaves behind the sensual and intuitive faculties in favour of abstract calculation—and is what got the mouse into trouble. We ignore the realm of the carnal at our peril. The realm of the senses, of touch, taste, smell—we've left it behind us. Philosophy is in a tight spot. I'm thinking here of Descartes, of course. Definitely a RIGHT FRONT man, as opposed, say, to a LEFT REAR.'

'Like me.'

'Yeah. Like Frank.'

Wart-Hog

Of all beasts, the wart-hog is the least modest in his claim to beauty. This African swine is not in a hurry. Eating or mating, he takes his time. Alone, he might pause and stand stock-still in the jungle: to close his eyes, and listen. From high up—filtering down through shade and sunshine—trill the songs of birds. Monkeys interrupt. And then the long calls descend in tremolos; before ascending to repeat their fall.

From under the wart-hog's cloven hooves, the pungence of dung and damp earth wafts up to his warty nostrils. He breathes his fill, and exhales with a soft whistle through his snout.

His beady eyes now open, the connoisseur lifts his gaze to the jungle flowers with their many colours—fuchsia and ochre, madder pink, chrome yellow, xanthene. Above, leaves flutter in a canopy: leaves *emeraude* and viridian, leaves of the greens parrot and pistachio; cloven leaves in lapping profusion as the jungle breathes and exhales. The wart-hog, struck dumb, is rooted to the spot.

Making a perfect target.

Yet his thick hide, a dull army-green, repels the arrow. Even so, arrow or bullet, the wart-hog has been blessed with further protection. The very sight of him—stunted tusks, piggy eyes, wart-like excrescences erupted on his snout—incites in the hunter, at the critical moment, such a tremor of repulsion as precludes a true aim.

Proving the Creator, also, has a weakness for beauty.

Hart-Royale

Once a stag has been chased by royalty—and escapes—he assumes a new dignity, a new name. He is known ever after as a hart-royale.

Scenes of the chase can be found in Persian miniatures—exquisite illuminated paintings from which the stag has yet to find exit. He prances on tiny hooves in the foreground, pursued by a pack of baying hounds with lolling tongues; the Shah's party brings up the rear, riding elephants with jewelled saddles and curtained chairs. Faded.

The past is so far away. It lives in another country, where once in a chariot, a King of France chased a stag as far as the Russian steppes, before turning back from a blizzard.

The wheels of the chariot rolled through mud. Mud much as our own mud, today; common mud, the kind that freezes into ruts and holds that shape for the rest of the winter. If something last-minute is needed from the store, one is forced to drive within rigid parallels—the old wheel-ruts from November and the first freeze.

The bitter cold. How do the deer survive it? With no cloaks to cover their shoulders, except the snow that falls, flake by flake, as the herd gathers at roadside; to nibble on salt. Ah but the rubies! ... Rubies for eyes! Dazzling red rubies lifted in pairs to the glare of your headlights. With a start, the deer, wheeling, returns them to the forest and the King of France.

The Gold Horn

Midnight, 1802 A.D. A goldsmith, having fashioned himself a key, opens the Royal Curio Cabinet. Holding his breath, he extracts the Gold Horn. In his workshop that night, he melts down the gold for jewellery.
    The following morning, King Frederick VII jails the goldsmith. He then consults an old manuscript in his library: a record of every precious object belonging to the crown. Within the heavy tome he turned to the old diagrams; the recovered gold is duly recast, and again scratched with tiny figures, moons ...

Morning, 1641 A.D. Olaf Worm, Artist to the Court, sits with his sketchbook balanced on his knees, on a stool in front of the Royal Curio Cabinet. The Gold Horn—discovered in a marsh and surrendered to the Crown of Denmark—lies within, locked behind glass: *Gold, 7½ kilos, 5th Century A.D.* Dutifully, Olaf Worm sketches what he sees as the ignorance of the distant past. He copies down the tiny figures engraved into the gold,
    two sea-serpents, nursing
    a three-headed woman
    a hedgehog kissing his mate
    an archer shooting at stars
    ... and so on; a bestiary from man's childhood.

Afternoon, 1639 A.D. With her peat-knife, Kirsten Svensdatter cuts through moss and grass roots; and rolls back a brick of peat, dripping and wet. The girl sits back on her heels. Wind off the North Sea shivers the grasses of the marsh. She bends to cut another square of peat, pulling back the flap—and a flash of gold winks up from the mud.
    A cloud obscures the sun.
    As the cloud moves on, reflected sunshine flashes into

Kirsten's eyes. She blinks, and leans forward for a closer look. Her braids wick up the waters of the bog as she digs carefully with her peat-knife.

The long sweep of the Horn extends the full measure of her arms. The Horn is heavy—Kirsten tugs it from the bog—and its mouth is filled with mud. She splashes water over its length, and down its throat. Pulling the Horn onto her lap, she sees that many small figures have been scratched into the gold. With a wet braid she rubs away the last of the mud, and dries the gold with her apron hem.

For hours, she studies the pictures:

Sea-serpents Kirsten has heard of, and thus is careful to swim close to shore. But a mare's teats are on her belly, not her back. And though most people have only a single head, Kirsten's mother is just like the lady pictured: she has one head to look behind her, one head which she bows to the hearth and the fixing of supper; and one head nodding sideways on her shoulder, eyes closed.

A pair of hedgehogs might kiss—it's possible.

And the archer shooting at stars could be her father, who sometimes late at night and giving no explanation, wanders out with his bow.

Kirsten Svensdatter traces the outline of a bullock with her finger: now she knows how the moon rises in the sky. She traces over the other engravings until she knows them by heart. Courage gathered, she leans over and presses her lips to the Horn's cold mouth. Her breath is still fragrant with milk from her morning's bowl. She blows gently into the Gold Horn, mindful of what she might summon to life; blows, and expels a long, desolate wail which quavers across the peat-bog.

The grasses shiver.

Again the girl purses her mouth to blow—after first brushing away tears, which had sprung unbidden at hearing the Horn's deep sadness, its wish for company.

At the second sounding of the Horn, the frogs of the marsh pulse in concert, croaking as if evening were drawing near, and twilight come upon us.

Twilight, 5th Century A.D. From now until dark, the stars will remain shot from the sky. An antlered man treads home across the marsh, arrows spent. He has yet to be scented by the grazing mare—whose foals float above her in rapture as they suckle.

Slowly the sun sinks.

And slowly, a bullock lifts his head, lifts the horns of the crescent moon: golden it rises, above a North Sea writhing with serpents.

The Dog Who Will Make All the Difference

Famous in children's literature is the Imaginary Dog, the one who will make all the difference. One morning he appears at the foot of the bed. Perhaps the child has been sick, and now lies weak from the empty thoughts which can propagate in the convalescent child—swelling her belly, hollowing her chest.

She stares out the third-floor window of the hospital, at the boughs of a swaying eucalyptus. Her arms lie atop the bedclothes, where the nurse has placed them.

It takes some time, but finally the child understands what the tree outside, scratching at the pane, has been trying to tell her, trying to point to: *Look.*

She turns her head. The dog at the foot of the bed wags his tail. He is bluish in colour, and transparent, you can see the furniture through him. He is wagging his tail and yawning with excitement: eager for their story to begin.

The Black Bull

His testicles hang pendulous with the weight of old coins
withheld from circulation, hoarded in a cinched leather sac
and swinging low to the ground;
old Chinese coins with a hole in the middle.

He tosses his head, shakes it and the mask of flies
lifts. Hovering, again it settles upon his face, flies crawling
around his blinking lids. The mask of the Personality.

He stares into the vacancy of the hour. A shudder
travels down his flank, a passing impulse. In his third stomach
    as in the Third Eye
revolve the grasses of his youth.

The Master's brush dips again into the inkstone:
against a blue wash of sky, his black tail
flicks with easy strokes
the characters for *Anger,* and *The Roof of the Mouth.*

The Great Shape-Shifter

More firemen in yellow slickers arrive, dragging fresh hoses across the schoolyard of St. Mary's.

The serpent trapped inside the three-storey brick convent has expanded to a crackling roar. Its orange-red scales press against every window as the reptile doubles over upon itself, swelling, until *POP POP POP, POP-POP-POP-POP!*—the glass of the windowpanes bursts into shards and explodes outwards.

The serpent next appears high above the rafters. The roof is gone, replaced with the fire's writhing neck, rising up as if from the centre of the earth. And this is all it had wanted: a creek's worth of water. From each fireman's hose, water arcs high into the air, to merge and drop in a single cataract into the serpent's maw: and be swallowed, the serpent swallowing its own tail. After several hours, having drunk its fill, it sinks hissing into the blackened ruins.

Across the schoolyard, the girls from First Grade, wearing pleated uniforms and supervised by nuns, line up at the water fountain. Each girl, when it comes her turn, bends down over the white basin and the porcelain ball at its centre. With one hand holding back her ringlets, she twists on the faucet: and to her lips leaps a flicking tail of water.

From a navel in the white ball it spurts up, wavering side to side.

The waterspout rises and sinks, rises and falls back with every twist of the fountain's valve. The water is cold. Some of the children splash it over their heat-reddened cheeks, dabbing at their singed eyebrows; and then take a last gulp under the nun's sharp eye before giving up their place in line—to the next girl, whose braids swing forward, as she bows down to the great Shape-shifter.

Diana Hartog immigrated to Canada in 1971, having received a B.A. and an M.A. from San Francisco State University. Divorced, she has a grown daughter, and lives in the Slocan Valley in British Columbia. Her two previous books of poetry are *Matinee Light* and *Candy From Strangers,* both from Coach House Press.

Editor for the Press: Michael Ondaatje
Design: Christopher Wadsworth / Reactor
Cover Painting: *Vietnam* by Jim Paterson

Coach House Press
401 (rear) Huron Street
Toronto, Canada
M5S 2G5